This is Tsutsui. Astonishingly, this is volume 15!

Thank you for supporting the series into a region where the fingers of both hands and one foot have to be utilized to count up the volumes!

When this volume came out in Japan in January 2020, it was also the time of year for the national entrance exam.

This is the final year of the current national entrance exam system. As a former exam taker, this development sparked some deep emotions.

To this year's test takers, I know it's a very challenging period. Please take good care of your health for the final sprint! I'm cheering you on from the shadows!

I hope you'll enjoy this love comic every now and then—in little sips during the exam breaks and in full, indulgent draughts for non-test takers!

• Taishi Tsutsui •

We Never Learn

We Never Learn

Volume 15 • SHONEN JUMP Manga Edition

STORY AND ART **Taishi Tsutsui**

TRANSLATION Camellia Nieh
SHONEN JUMP SERIES LETTERING Snir Aharon
GRAPHIC NOVEL TOUCH-UP ART & LETTERING Erika Terriquez
DESIGN Shawn Carrico
EDITOR John Bae

BOKUTACHI WA BENKYOU GA DEKINAI © 2017 by Taishi Tsutsui
All rights reserved.
First published in Japan in 2017 by SHUEISHA Inc., Tokyo.
English translation rights arranged by SHUEISHA Inc.

The stories, characters and incidents mentioned in this publication are entirely fictional.

No portion of this book may be reproduced or transmitted in any form
or by any means without written permission from the copyright holders.

Printed in Canada

Published by VIZ Media, LLC
P.O. Box 77010
San Francisco, CA 94107

10 9 8 7 6 5 4 3 2 1
First printing, April 2021

PARENTAL ADVISORY
WE NEVER LEARN is rated T+ for Older Teen and is recommended for ages 16 and up. This volume contains mild language and sexual themes.

[x] We Never Learn
15
More than Ever, What Supports [X] Is...
Taishi Tsutsui
Central Islip Public Library
33 Hawthorne Avenue
Central Islip, NY 11722

We Never Learn

Characters & Story

Nariyuki Yuiga and his family have led a humble life since his father passed away, with Yuiga doing everything he can to support his siblings. So when the principal of his school agrees to grant Nariyuki the school's special VIP recommendation for a full scholarship to college, he leaps at the opportunity. However, the principal's offer comes with one condition: Yuiga must serve as the tutor of Rizu Ogata, Fumino Furuhashi and Uruka Takemoto, the three girl geniuses who are the pride of Ichinose Academy! Unfortunately, the girls, while extremely talented in certain ways, all have subjects where their grades are absolutely rock-bottom. How will these three struggling students ever manage to pass their college entrance exams?!

To combat Rizu's self-loathing, Nariyuki shows her an essay in which Fumino writes about her admiration of Rizu. And as Rizu comes to understand her late-grandmother's kindness, she also realizes she has romantic feelings for Nariyuki! Meanwhile, the new year is beginning, which means the national exam is coming up!

A bright student from an ordinary family. Nariyuki lacks genius in any one subject but manages to maintain stellar grades through hard work. Agrees to take on the role of tutor in return for the school's special VIP recommendation.

CLASS:3-B

☺ Liberal Arts
☺ STEM
☹ Athletics

The Yuiga Family

A family of five, consisting of Nariyuki, his mother and his siblings, Mizuki, Hazuki and Kazuki.

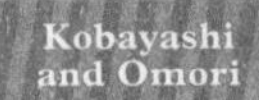

Nariyuki's friends.

Sawako Sekijo

The head of the science club and a rival of Rizu's, who in fact adores Rizu.

Kawase and Umihara

Uruka's friends.

The Principal

Appoints Nariyuki as the girls' tutor.

RIZU OGATA

CLASS:3-F

☹ Liberal Arts ☺ STEM ☹ Athletics

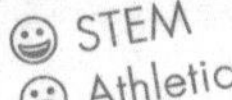

Known as the Thumbelina Supercomputer, Rizu is a math and science genius, but she's a dunce at literature, especially when human emotions come into play. She chooses a literary path to learn about human psychology—partially because she wants to become better at board games.

FUMINO FURUHASHI

CLASS:3-A

☺ Liberal Arts ☹ STEM ☺ Athletics

Known as the Sleeping Beauty of the Literary Forest, Fumino is a literary wiz whose mind goes completely blank when she sees numbers. She chooses a STEM path because she wants to study the stars.

URUKA TAKEMOTO

CLASS:3-D

☹ Liberal Arts ☹ STEM ☺ Athletics

Known as the Shimmering Ebony Mermaid Princess, Uruka is a swimming prodigy but is terrible at academics. In order to get an athletic scholarship, she needs to meet certain academic standards. She's had a crush on Nariyuki since junior high.

MAFUYU KIRISU

TEACHER

☺ Pedagogy

☹ Home Economics

A teacher at Ichinose Academy, and Rizu and Fumino's previous tutor. She believes people should choose their path according to their talents.

ASUMI KOMINAMI

OG

☹ Science

☺ Service

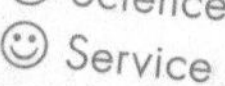

A graduate of Ichinose Academy. Works at a maid cafe and attends cram school in order to get into medical school and take over her father's clinic one day.

TITLE

We Never Learn

CONTENTS

VOLUME **15** More than Ever, What Supports [*X*] Is...

NAME Taishi Tsutsui

Question 124: Sometimes a Genius's Transformation Becomes a Great Leap in [X]

STUDY HALL

1/2

16 MORE DAYS UNTIL THE NATIONAL EXAM!

SKRIT SKRIT

SKRIT SKRIT

NARI-YUKI...

THE VERB IRU...

...IS IN THE UPPER MONO-GRADE CLASS OF VERBS, RIGHT?

YES, OGATA...

THERE'S A USEFUL MNEMONIC FOR RE-MEMBER-ING UPPER MONO-GRADE VERBS...

?
IS SOME-THING WRONG...
...NARI-YUKI?
National Exam Language Arts
LANGUAGE ARTS
OH...
NOTH-ING'S WRONG.
JUST, UH...
DID YOU CHANGE SOMETHING ABOUT YOURSELF RECENTLY?
I KNOW! YOUR HAIR-STYLE!
DID YOU CHANGE YOUR HAIR-STYLE?!
You're styling it in a new way!
WELL DONE!
I HAVE BETTER VISIBILITY THIS WAY, AND IT'S EASIER TO STUDY!
OH! I SEE!
Nice!

YOU GOT 12.5 PERCENT.

HUH?
YOU ASKED ME IF I CHANGED SOMETHING.
YOUR GUESS WAS 12.5 PERCENT RIGHT.
CAN YOU GUESS THE OTHER 87.5 PERCENT?

HUH?
WHAT?
THEN AGAIN...
MAYBE I'M ASKING TOO MUCH.

YOU'RE KINDA DENSE WHEN IT COMES TO THIS STUFF, NARIYUKI.
WHAT ...?

BRING IT ON, OGATA!
I GOT THIS IN THE BAG!
GREAT! THAT'S THE SPIRIT, NARIYUKI!

SOBA
BA
UDON
TADANO DINER
THERE AREN'T A LOT OF PLACES OPEN.
WELL, PLACES ARE STILL CLOSED FOR NEW YEAR'S.
I HOPE WE CAN FIND SOMEWHERE CHEAP THAT'S OPEN...
UNFORTUNATELY WE'RE ALL OUT OF THE GOOD STUFF AT MY PLACE...
RRMBL
I'm hungry!
Yeah...
AND WHEN I SAY GOOD STUFF, I MEAN UDON!
...
YEAH, SOMETHING'S DIFFERENT ABOUT OGATA LATELY.
EVER SINCE CHRISTMAS...

...SHE SEEMS GENTLER, SOMEHOW.

AND, UNLESS I'M IMAGINING IT...

...SHE'S SMILING MORE THAN SHE USED TO.

I WAS KINDA WORRIED, BUT...

...I'M GLAD SHE'S FEELING BETTER.

SHF...

LET'S DO IT!

DUM
WHAT?! JUST LIKE THAT?!
I MEAN, THAT'S NOT SOME-THING YOU JUST DECIDE ALL OF A SUDDEN, YOU KNOW...
?
HUH? WHY'RE YOU FREAK-ING OUT?
SHP

MOCHI POUNDING SIGN-IN
Saegusa Shopping Arcade
NEW YEAR'S MOCHI POUNDING EVENT!
CHATTER CHATTER CHATTER
WHAK WHAK
OZONI 250 YEN
KINAKO MOCHI 200 YEN
ANKO MOCHI 200 YEN

DDDDUH
IT'S ALWAYS BEEN A DREAM OF MINE...
...TO BE TOGETHER WITH SOMEONE AND POUND MOCHI!
YAY!
BLUSH
WHO TALKS LIKE THAT?!
SO CONFUSING...
!
FWAH

HEY... WHAT'S THAT SCENT?
SORT OF CITRUSY...
A FRESH, SWEET FRAGRANCE...

OGATA...
ARE YOU WEARING PERFUME?
!

NOW YOU'RE 25 PERCENT RIGHT.
THIS AROMA'S SUPPOSED TO HAVE A RELAXING EFFECT...
...AND ALSO SUPPORT MEMORY RETENTION.

WOW!
YOU'RE SO DEDICATED TO LEARNING!
Yay! Another good guess! ♪
NOW THAT YOU MENTION IT, IT IS KINDA SOOTHING...
SNIFF SNIFF

IF YOU SAY YES...
...THEN I'LL WEAR IT WHENEVER WE SEE EACH OTHER.
YEAH, I LIKE IT!
UM... WE'RE STILL TALKING ABOUT THE PER-FUME ...
... RIGHT?
HEH HEH!
SO, LET'S DO IT TOGETHER.
YOU'RE TALKING ABOUT MOCHI POUNDING, RIGHT?!
RIGHT?!
Saegusa Shopping Arcade
NEW YEAR'S MOCHI POUNDING EVENT!
MOCHI POUNDING SIGN-IN
OZONI 250 YEN
KINAKO MOCHI 200 YEN
ANKO MOCHI 200 YEN

SHOOSH
HARRR...
RRUMF...
WOBBLE WOBBLE
QUIVER
WOBBLE
OGATAAAAAA!!
HOW MORTIFYING...
HFF HFF
HOW WEAK CAN YOU GET?!
Not that I'm one to talk...
WANT ME TO TAKE OVER?
N-NO...
UM...
IF YOU DON'T MIND...
...HOW ABOUT ...?
?
WHSHH

SPLAK

SPLAK
SPLAK
OMG! WE'RE SO CLOSE!
AND EVERY-ONE'S WATCH-ING US!
THIS IS SO MOVING, NARI-YUKI!
IT'S LIKE A DREAM!
A DREAM COME TRUE!
WELL... IF IT REALLY MAKES OGATA HAPPY...
...THAT'S WHAT MAT-TERS...
Wow... she smells good...
...

BOING BOING
BUT...
...IT'S REALLY HARD TO KNOW WHERE TO LOOK.
Even through her coat...
OH!
NAIL POLISH?
What a pretty color!
!
NOW YOU'VE GUESSED...
...37.5 PERCENT!

SO...

PSYCHOLO-
GISTS HAVE
FOUND
THAT THE
COLOR BLUE
SUPPORTS
INCREASED
CONCENTRA-
TION.

IT'S A PURELY RATIONAL CHOICE...

...TO KEEP THE COLOR BLUE IN MY FIELD OF VISION WHILE STUDY-ING!

I GET IT!

I GUESS THERE ARE ALL SORTS OF WAYS TO ENHANCE OUR STUDIES!

THANKS FOR EDUCAT-ING ME!

HMPH!

EVEN HAVING BLUE...

....WITHIN MY FIELD OF VISION DIDN'T HELP ME FOCUS AT ALL!

She's so close!

Boing boing

SLRRP SLRRP

SLRRP SLRRP

PHEW! THAT WARMED ME UP!

I'M ALMOST HOT NOW!

FWIP FWIP

RIGHT...

WELL, IT WAS CERTAINLY A WORK-OUT POUND-ING THAT MOCHI!

NARI-YUKI...

HERE.

IF YOU DON'T WIPE YOUR SWEAT, YOU COULD CATCH A CHILL!

BLRF

OH... RIGHT!
THANKS, OGATA...
!

A NECK-
LACE!
SHOOP
THAT...
THAT'S NEW TOO, ISN'T IT?!

YES.
NOW YOU'VE REACHED 50 PER-
CENT!
YES!

THIS NECK-
LACE IS MAG-
NETIC.
IT'S SUPPOSED TO HELP RELIEVE SHOULDER TENSION FROM STUDYING.
WOW! ANOTHER ITEM TO HELP WITH STUDYING!
Who knew?

SO...
HOW...
...DO I SEEM TO YOU TODAY?

UM...
LIKE A VERY DILIGENT AND MOTIVATED STUDENT?

SHOOP

IS THAT ALL?

C-CLOSE!

YOU'RE TOO CLOSE AGAIN, OGATA!

IS...

... THAT ALL?

STARE

YOU SEEM MORE FEMININE SOME-HOW...
AND...
...VERY PRETTY.
BLUSH
S-SO...
WHEN YOU GET TOO CLOSE, I GET SELF-CONSCIOUS!
COULD YOU TRY TO BE MORE AWARE OF THAT?!
PLEASE ?!

SORRY. THAT'S OVER NOW.
K'CHAM
WHAA-AT?!
C'MON, DON'T LEAVE ME HANGING LIKE THAT!
GIVE ME SOME CLUES!
SORRY. ALL DONE! ♪
BECAUSE...
...YOU ALREADY...
...SAID ALL THE RIGHT ANSWERS!

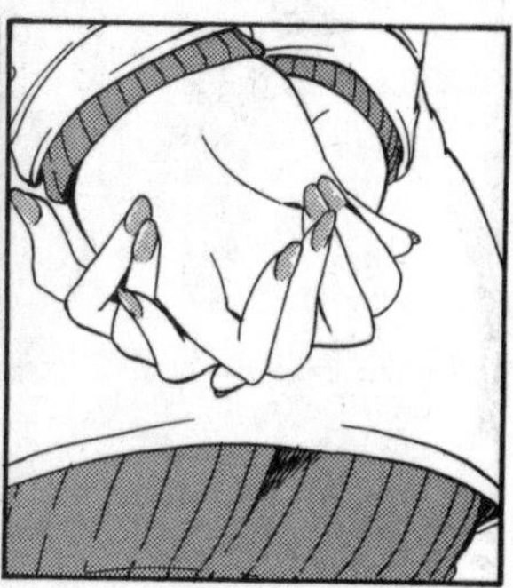

FIFTY PERCENT OF THE ANSWER PERTAINED TO PHYSICAL CHANGES RELATED TO STUDYING.

YOU SEEM MORE FEMININE SOME-HOW...

AND VERY PRETTY.

BUT THE OTHER 50 PER-CENT...

...HAS TO DO WITH HOW I FEEL...

...WHEN A CERTAIN CLUELESS SOMEONE SAYS THOSE THINGS TO ME!

SPURT
SPURT

I would've scored 100 percent easy!

Rizu Ogata, you're a goddess...

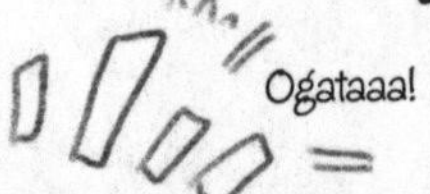
Ogataaa!

Question 125: A Young Girl's Acts of Devotion to [X]

TIK
TIK
TIK

NOD NOD
NOD NOD
zzZ

SHOO SHOO
GLEAM

BAM
TUG
HEALING MUSIC
RELAXING AROMATHERAPY OILS
SHOOOSH
THUMP
THUMP
THUMP
THUMP
THUMP
THUMP
THUMP
TWEET
TWEET

WHOA!
I'VE BEEN PULLING LOTSA LATE NIGHTS LATELY...
...BUT I WOKE UP THIS MORNING FEELING GREAT! AS IF I'D SLEPT TEN HOURS!
Good morning, big bro!
Let's play!
SPARKLE SPARKLE
WELL, THAT'S WONDER-FUL!
PLEASED TO MEET YOU. I'M MIZUKI YUIGA.
YUIGA'S YOUNGER SISTER!
NAIJO NO KOU
AND I'M COMMITTED TO DOING EVERYTHING IN MY POWER TO SUPPORT MY BIG BROTHER LEADING UP TO HIS EXAMS!
THANKS FOR THE FOOD! I'M OFF TO CRAM SCHOOL!
WAIT A SECOND! YOUR HAIR'S STICKING UP! HAVE YOU GOT YOUR HANDKER-CHIEF AND TISSUES?
ANYONE SEEN MY WORK CLOTHES?
RUSH RUSH
THEY'RE SOME-WHERE IN YOUR DRESSER!
SO DIF-FER-ENT!
IF I SEE A WAY I CAN HELP MY BROTHER ...
...I'LL DO IT!

OH NO!
HE FOR-GOT HIS LUNCH!

SAEGUSA SEMINAR
NO.1 RESULTS
SAEGUSA SEMINAR

S- SO THIS IS CRAM SCHOOL ...
GLANCE GLANCE
GOSH, I FEEL NERVOUS.
BUT A GOOD SISTER MAKES SURE HER BROTHER EATS!

BUT HOW CAN I GET IT TO HIM?
I CAN'T JUST WALK IN, CAN I?
HM...
HEY!
!
WHAT ARE YOU DOING OUT HERE?
CLASS IS STARTING! GET TO YOUR SEAT!
?
EEK!
JOLT
WHY...
WHY IS THIS HAP-PENING?!
SKRIT
SKRIT
SKRIT
SKRIT

CHATTER
CHATTER
CHATTER

NOBODY DISTURBS MY BROTHER'S SCHOOL-WORK...
DA DA DA
DA
DUM
Eek!
Eek!
WHA-AAT?!
M-MIZUKI?!
WHAT'RE YOU DOING HERE?!
OOPS! I DIDN'T MEAN TO...
MAY I CONTINUE WITH THE LESSON?

SO, YOU'RE KOHAI'S LITTLE SISTER!

NICE TO MEET YOU!

SPARKLE

I HEAR YOU WERE BATTLING EVIL IN THE CLASS-ROOM!

NICE WORK, MIZUKI! Want a doughnut?

SPARKLE

LONG TIME NO SEE, MIZUKI!

HAVE SOME UDON!

OH!

THANK YOU!

SHEESH...

WHY'RE THERE SO MANY GIRLS?
DROOP
DA DA DA
DA DUM
Yum!
Is it good?
AND THEY'RE ALL SUPER BEAUTIFUL!
IS THIS HOW BIG BROTHER ALWAYS STUDIES?

WOW... YOU CAME ALL THIS WAY TO BRING HIS LUNCH?
YOU'RE A GOOD SISTER, MIZUKI!
YES, SHE'S AN AMAZING SISTER.
THANK YOU FOR ALL THAT YOU DO, MIZUKI!
Tee hee!
WELL...
TAKE-MOTO SENPAI GETS SPECIAL STATUS!
HEH HEH HEH...

NARIYUKI! NARIYUKI!
WHAT DOES THIS WORD MEAN?
KANASHI... IS THAT LIKE KANASHII (SAD)?
SHP
ACTUALLY, IT MEANS "DEAR."
!

UM, NARI-YUKI...
I'M HAVING TROUBLE SOLVING THIS PROB-LEM...
!!
Saegusa Seminar
MATHEMATICS

SORRY, KOHAI.
COULD YOU HAVE A LOOK AT THIS TOO?
!!!

WELL, FURUHASHI, YOU'RE USING THE WRONG EQUATION HERE.
USE THE TRIPLE ANGLE FORMULA...
Mm-hm!
Mm-hm!
AND, YOU, SENPAI...
Hmm!
DA DA DA DUH
YUIGA! HELP!
...

CHATTER CHATTER

Grr

BIG BROTHER, LOOK!
HERE'S THE LUNCH I PACKED YOU...

OH!
SORRY, MIZU-KI...
DO YOU MIND WAITING JUST A BIT?

MIZUKI...
I PROMISE...
...I WON'T LET YOU BE LONELY!

ALL THIS TIME...
...HE WAS...
...ALWAYS JUST...
...OUR BIG BROTHER

I JUST REMEMBERED! THERE'S A SPECIAL SUPERMARKET SALE TODAY!
I'D BETTER GET GOING!
!

WAIT, MIZUKI!
SEE YOU LATER!
THANKS FOR THE UDON AND THE DOUGHNUT!
KCHAM
OH! TOO BAD...
SHE COULD'VE AT LEAST STAYED AND HAD LUNCH WITH US...

!

KUSUMOTO PARK
SIGH...
THERE WAS NO SUPER-MARKET SALE.
WHY DID I LIE?
SQUEAK
SQUEAK
...
MAYBE BIG BROTHER...
... DOESN'T NEED ME ANY-MORE.
WAH!
WAH!
DADDY ...
DADDY ...

YOU'RE STILL OUT HERE, MIZUKI?
LET'S HEAD HOME.
I'M NOT A GREAT COOK, BUT I'LL DO MY BEST TO MAKE US DINNER!
I DON'T WANT ANY.
I DON'T WANNA GO HOME.
WHAT'S THE POINT!
DADDY'S GONE!
TMP
KREAK
!
KREAK
KREAK
?
BROTHER?
DAD USED TO DO THIS A LOT, DIDN'T HE?
RIDING DOUBLES ON THE SWINGS!

I'LL MAKE UP FOR DAD BEING GONE!

MIZUKI...

I PROMISE...

...I WON'T LET YOU BE LONELY!

YOU STILL HAVE YOUR BROTHER!

SO DON'T WORRY!

GOT THAT?

EVERYTHING'S GOING TO BE OKAY!

EVER SINCE THAT DAY...
...BIG BROTHER'S WORKED SO HARD FOR OUR FAMILY.
IT'S NOT FAIR OF ME...
...TO BE JEALOUS...

MIZU-KI!

HUFF
HUFF

BIG BROTH-ER!
WHAT'RE YOU DOING HERE?
WHAT ?!

I PROMISED YOU, RE-MEMBER?
I CAN'T LEAVE MY LITTLE SISTER ALONE...
...WHEN YOU LOOK SO SAD!
SO...
DO YOU MIND IF I KEEP YOU COM-PANY?
HUH?
BADMP
BADMP
BIG BROTH-ER...
...YOU MEAN ...

KREAK
KREAK

...
WHAT'RE YOU DOING?!
WHAT? ISN'T IT OBVI-OUS?
WE USED TO DO THIS A LOT, REMEM-BER?
KREAK KREAK KREAK

I'VE BEEN SO BUSY STUDY-ING LATELY THAT I HAVEN'T BEEN PAYING MUCH ATTENTION TO YOU.
WHEN EXAMS ARE OVER...
...I'LL HAVE A BIT MORE TIME TO PLAY.

TIME TO PLAY?
YOU KNOW, BIG BROTH-ER...
I'M NOT A KID ANY-MORE!

WHAT DOES THAT MATTER?

EVEN WHEN WE'RE OLD AND GRAY...
...I'LL STILL BE YOUR BIG BROTHER, RIGHT?
I'LL ALWAYS BE HERE FOR YOU, SO DON'T HIDE YOUR FEELINGS!

WELL...
I GUESS YOU'LL GET MARRIED AT SOME POINT...
AW...
...SO YOU PROBABLY WON'T NEED ME AS MUCH...

OH!
AND AN-OTHER THING!

THAT LUNCH...
...WITH PORK CUTLETS ...
...RICE BALLS WITH CHERRY-BLOSSOM STARCH...
...AND SAUSAGES ...
...WAS REALLY DELICIOUS AND THOUGHTFUL!

HA HA HA!
GOOD ONE!
HA HA HA HA
C'MON, WE'RE NOT KIDS ANYMORE!
KRIK

Oh... But...
BADMP
He'll always be there for me... In a way that sounds like...
Isn't this even more than what an average wife can expect?!

Question 126:
A Predecessor Stockpiles [X] in Anticipation of the Big Day
DING-A-LING-A-LING-A-LING
YOU WIN!
KTUNK KTUNK
HUH?
HOW COME I GOT TWO?
WOW! YOU WON, ASHUMI!
I'VE NEVER SEEN THAT BE-FORE!
...
HERE, HAVE THESE, MACHIKO!
HUH?
BOTH OF THEM?!
SHUP
HOW COME?!

ASHUMI...
YOU'RE REALLY CUTE SOMETIMES, YOU KNOW THAT? ♪
OH...
PUHLEASE!!

HUH?
IT'S KOMINAMI SENPAI AND MACHIKO!
!
HEY, KOHAI!
HI! HAVEN'T SEEN YOU SINCE NEW YEAR'S!
WHAT A COINCIDENCE, RUNNING INTO YOU HERE!

SHEESH... THAT MACHIKO!

WELL, SINCE WE'RE BOTH HERE...

LET'S FIND A PLACE TO DO SOME STUDYING.

福引

CHATTER CHATTER

LUCK-OF-THE-DRAW SPIN

!

OH!

DO YOU MIND IF I HAVE A GO?

BAM

LUCK OF THE DRAW, HUH?
THANKS FOR WAITING FOR ME.
MY MOM GAVE ME A TICKET FOR THIS.
LUCK-OF-THE-DRAW

Ha ha ha
HOPE I GET SOMETHING PRACTICAL, LIKE TISSUES OR TOILET PAPER...
That's kinda sad.
CLATTER
CLATTER
PLONK
YAAAAY!
DING-A
LING-A
LING-A
WE HAVE A BIG WIN-NER!!

OUR GRAND PRIZE ...
FREE TICKETS TO DOHA-CHAN LAND!
1ST PRIZE
DOHA-CHAN LAND
WHAAAAAT?!

NO WAY!
OOOOH!
DOHA-CHAN!
LUCKY!
THAT'S AMAZ-ING!!
...
HERE, SENPAI!

YOU TAKE THESE!
THEY'RE GOOD FOR HALF A YEAR.
YOU CAN GO AFTER EXAMS ARE OVER!
WHAT?! FOR REAL?!

GASP
ZOOP
EXAM DAY LUCK SCALE

N-NOTH-ING!
IT'S NOTHING, REALLY!
STUDY TIME! LET'S GET TO WORK!
RAWR!
WHUT?!
GIRLS ARE SO CONFUS-ING!

Jomothan's
Jomothan's
COFFEE & RESTAURANT

UM...
ARE YOU SURE?
YEAH.
I CAN TAKE CARE OF MYSELF, KOHAI. YOU WORRY ABOUT YOURSELF, YOUNG WHIPPER-SNAPPER!
I'VE GOTTA REPLENISH SOME OF MY LUCK...
MUTTER
?
EXAM DAY LUCK SCALE

TING-A LING-A LING
CON-GRAT-ULA-TIONS!

TADAAA

YOU'RE OUR 100TH CUS-TOMER TODAY!

100TH CUSTOMER

YOU WIN A FREE DESSERT!

FREE DESSERT

WOW, NICE ONE, SENPAI!

AAAA-AGH!

BLOOP

EXAM DAY LUCK SCALE

OH, GREAT! THEY GAVE US THE BEST TABLE FOR STUDY-ING!

DA DA DA DUM

A CORNER BOOTH RIGHT BY A WIN-DOW!

DA DA-DUM

AND RIGHT WHEN I ASK FOR MORE RICE...

...A BRAND-NEW BATCH IS READY!

Hup!♪

STEAM

STEAM

DA DA DA DA DUM

CHING

YOUR CHANGE IS 777 YEN!

YOUR CHANGE

777 YEN

AAA-AAH!

DA DA DA DUM

BAM
BLOOP
BLOOP
EXAM DAY
LUCK
SCALE

WHAT ON EARTH IS GOING ON...?
WORMP
SENPAI!!

WHAT'S WITH YOU TODAY?
IF SOMETHING'S BOTHERING YOU, YOU CAN TELL ME!
NO... IT'S NOTHING...

NUZZLE
HM?
...

SQUEAK! ♡

PLEASE, DON'T MOVE!

JUST STAY WITH ME LIKE THIS FOR A MOMENT...

SQUEAK!
N-NOOO! I CAN'T!!
SENPAI!!
SHOOSH

ROLL
OH!
OH...
SPLOSH
AAA-AUGH! OH NO!!

SHAAA

OOOH... SO COLD ...

I THOUGHT I WAS A GONER...

THIRTY MINUTES EARLIER...
SEN-PAI!!
SEN-PAI!!
I...
I'M OKAY! I JUST GOT MY HEAD A LITTLE WET. NO BIGGIE...
TREMBL
TREMBL
IT'S NOT OKAY!
YOU COULD TOTALLY CATCH A COLD!
FWAP
!
?!
S
HUP
HEY! PUT ME DOWN!
NOPE. I'M TAKING YOU STRAIGHT HOME!
I CAN WALK!
PUT ME DOWN, YOU JERK! I'M GOING TO BE REALLY MAD AT YOU FOR THIS!
FINE. I DON'T MIND.
YOUR HEALTH MATTERS MORE TO ME!

SHAAA
...
HMPH. THAT KOHAI! PLAYING THE HERO...
EVEN THOUGH HE'S YOUNGER THAN ME!

BLOOP
EXAM DAY LUCK SCALE
HUH?
Weird... I just felt my luck scale move...

ASUMI
HUH?
FWOOO
YOU'RE TRYING TO SAVE UP YOUR LUCK FOR THE EXAM?

I SEE...
SO THAT'S WHY YOU WERE ACTING SO FUNNY TODAY.
FWOOO
YEAH...
SORRY FOR BEING SUCH A HANDFUL...
GO AHEAD, YOU CAN LAUGH AT ME. LIKE MACHIKO.
NO WAY.
I GET HOW YOU FEEL.
BUT, SENPAI...
YOU KNOW, YOU'RE PRETTY CUTE SOMETIMES!
BLOOP
EXAM DAY LUCK SCALE

AUGH!!
SEE?! YOU ARE LAUGHING AT ME, YOU CHEEKY RUNT!
AND I CAN DRY MY OWN HAIR, THANK YOU!
DA DA DA DA DUM
OH! SORRY!
I JUST DON'T WANT YOU TO CATCH A COLD...

OH!
ALL RIGHT, I'LL GO MAKE SOME TEA!
Warm you up on the inside!
SHOOSH
HUH?!

NO, IT'S OKAY!
YOU REALLY DON'T HAVE TO DO THAT...
STOP!
SHOOP

!
WOBBLE

SEN-PAI, WATCH OUT!!
KRASH KRASH KRASH
YEEK!!
OOG...

NATIONAL EXAM
PRACTICE TESTS
LANGUAGE ARTS
25

OUCH ...
SHOOF
YOU OKAY, SEN-PAI?!
PLOP
PLOP
YEAH ...
I'M SORRY ...
IT'S SUPER IMPORTANT TO TAKE CARE OF YOUR BODY RIGHT NOW WITH TESTS COMING UP!
BE CAREFUL, OKAY?
That was close!

ZOOOOOP

EXAM DAY
LUCK
SCALE

NO!
IT'S JUST BECAUSE YOU SAVED ME FROM GETTING HURT!
N-NOT FOR ANY OTHER REASON!!
AAAH!
HUH?!
WHAT ARE YOU TALKING ABOUT?!

IN THE END...
AAAAAH
Heya, toots!
BLOOPBLOOP
Can you really concentrate like that?
THANKS TO HAMMY'S HELP, MY LUCK RECOVERED NICELY!!

A kiss on the forehead?!!
HEARTBEAT ♡ GAUGE
BAZOOM

Question 127:
The [X]s Face the Fateful Morning Fresh and Pure!
LIBRARY
OH...
OH NO!!
THE NA-TIONAL EXAM IS COMING UP!!
DDDA DA DA
U...
UDON! HAVE SOME UDON AND CALM DOWN, FUMINO!
TREMBL
TREMBL
TREMBL
DUM
TAKE SOME DEEP BREATHS, BOTH OF YOU!
AND RIZURIN, WE'RE NOT ALLOWED TO EAT OR DRINK IN THE LIBRARY!
Aaah! Eeek! Augh!
...

OUR SHORT WINTER BREAK CAME AND WENT.
THE THIRD TERM IS HERE.
ONLY TEN DAYS REMAIN...
...UNTIL THE NATIONAL EXAM.

FUNDAMENTALLY, ADMISSIONS TO PUBLIC UNIVERSITIES...

...ARE BASED ON A NATIONAL EXAM HELD IN JANUARY...

...PLUS SECONDARY EXAMS FOR THE INDIVIDUAL UNIVERSITIES IN FEBRUARY AND MARCH.

NATIONAL EXAM IN JANUARY

+

SECONDARY EXAMS FOR EACH SCHOOL IN FEBRUARY OR MARCH

PASS

FAIL

WE'VE GOTTA GET THE HIGHEST SCORES POSSIBLE ON THAT NATIONAL EXAM...

I'VE GOT A STOMACHACHE FROM ALL THE STRESS... EVEN THOUGH OGATA AND FURUHASHI ARE PROBABLY FEELING IT EVEN WORSE...

Guh Guh Guh

OOOG... MY HANDS ARE TREMBLING...
I-IT'S OKAY. AFTER ALL, ON THE PRACTICE EXAM THE OTHER DAY...
RUSTLE
OH!
SHF
FWAP...
OH! SORRY...

JOLT
P-P-PRINCI-PAL?!
CARE-FUL, NOW.
S-S-SORRY!
...
I SAW THE RESULTS...
...FROM THE PRACTICE EXAM.

OH! WELL ...
I MEAN, THIS IS JUST...
Ha ha ha!
YOURS...
...OGATA'S, FURU-HASHI'S...
AND ...
TAKE-MOTO'S AS WELL.

IN APRIL ...
AFTER I AP-POINTED YOU AS THEIR TUTOR...
...I THOUGHT ...
...YOU WOULD CONVINCE THEM RIGHT AWAY TO CHANGE THEIR INTENDED FIELDS OF STUDY.
I THOUGHT IT WAS NECESSARY.
I THOUGHT THAT AS THEIR CLASS-MATE...
...THEY MIGHT BE MORE OPEN IN LISTENING TO YOU.
LESS RESIS-TANT.
FORGIVE ME.

I'M VERY IM-PRESSED.
YOU HELPED THEM OVERCOME THEIR OBSTACLES.
THAT'S QUITE AN ACHIEVE-MENT...
...YUIGA.

I...
...EN-JOYED IT.

SINCE THEY WORKED SO HARD TO OVER-COME...
...THE THINGS THEY COULDN'T DO...
...I WAS GLAD TO HELP.

I JUST SUP-PORT-ED THEM ...
...BE-CAUSE...
...IT FELT GOOD.
AND ...

THEY'RE THE ONES WHO OVERCAME THOSE HURDLES...
...BY THEIR OWN POWER.
NOTE
YUIGA...
LISTEN, YUIGA...
NOW, OF ALL TIMES, WHY DON'T YOU FORGET ABOUT YOUR STUDENTS...
...AND PRIORITIZE YOUR OWN HEALTH.
NO, IT'S OKAY.
I ENJOY SEEING THEM TRY SO HARD.

WELL, SURE, BUT...
I WORRY ABOUT ...
...MY ELDEST SON. HE CRIES A LOT.
YOU'RE MY BEST FRIEND, YOSHIMI.
I WANT HIM TO GO TO YOUR HIGH SCHOOL...
...SO THAT YOU CAN PROVIDE THE STRICT GUIDANCE HE NEEDS.

DO YOU SEE ...
... YUIGA ?
YOUR SON GREW UP STRONG AND CARING...
JUST LIKE YOU.
WELL ...
Koff
IT'S NOT OVER YET, AND THERE'S NO TELLING WHAT WILL HAPPEN...
...SO HANG IN THERE AND GIVE IT YOUR BEST TILL THE END!
R-RIGHT!

BLUSH

HEY... YOU ALL SEEM LOST IN YOUR OWN WORLDS TODAY...
ARE YOU NERVOUS ABOUT THE NATIONAL EXAM?
OH, IT'S NOT THAT...
SKWEEZ
HUH?!
NARI-YUKI...
YOUR HANDS ARE COLD!
PAT

LET ME WARM THEM UP FOR YOU.

AAAH!

M-ME TOO!

WHAT?!

I'LL HELP TOO!

PEOPLE ALWAYS SAY I HAVE WARM HANDS!

SHP

I MEAN, IT'S WINTER AND ALL! IT'S ONLY NATURAL, RIGHT?!

I-I-IT'S OKAY, YOU GUYS!

TH-THIS IS EMBARRASSING!

...

BOTH OF THEM...

...HAVE GOTTEN SURPRISINGLY BOLD LATELY.

BADMP BADMP

HEY, NARIYUKI! CHECK IT OUT!

A HEAT PACK! WANT ONE?!

HUH? YOU TOO, FURUHASHI?!

CROWD
WHAT?!
WHAT'S GOING ON?!
CROWD
CROWD
LOOK, MAMA! THEY'RE PLAYING THE HUGGING GAME!
HEE HEE ...
I HAD TO VIE FOR YOUR FATHER LIKE THAT BACK IN THE DAY! ♡

RRRIP

1/9

1/10

1/11

1/14
Mum's the word!
Lips sealed!
QUIET, PLEASE! STUDYING IN SESSION!

1/15
SUCCESS!

JANUARY 18...
NATIONAL EXAM TEST DAY
YOU'VE GOT THIS!
JUST DO YOUR THING, NARIYUKI!
DO YOU HAVE YOUR REGIS-TRATION SLIP, BIG BROTH-ER?
AND YOUR PENCIL BOX? AND YOUR TISSUES? AND...
BREAK A LEG, BIG BRO!
YEP, I'M GOOD!
SEE YOU LATER!

KRUNCH

SUPERWOMAN SUPERMARKET
WOW, THE SNOW'S PRETTY DEEP...
KRUNCH
SKF SKF
GOTTA BE CAREFUL NOT TO SLIP!
GLAD I LEFT EARLY!
BUT THE WEATHER'S NICE!
AND I FEEL GOOD!
IT'S A GREAT DAY FOR A TEST!
YIP YIP YIP
!
Pant Pant
YIP YIP
TAK TAK TAK TAK
BRRMMM

BRRRMMM
SHOOOSH
SKREEEEE
WATCH OUT!!
HUFF!
HUFF!
HUFF!
?
?
Phew...
THANK ...
THANK GOODNESS!
WHERE DO YOU LIVE, DOGGY?

SWF
WHOOSH
WHA-?!
ICHINOSE UNIVERSITY
NATIONAL EXAM

BAM
HEYA, RIZU-RIN!
FUMI-NOCCHI!

U-URUKA-CHAN?!
I THOUGHT YOU WEREN'T TAKING THE NATIONAL EXAM!
WELL, I CAME OUT TO CHEER YOU ON, OBVIOUSLY! ♪
GO TEAM!
NATIONAL EXAM

WOWZA!
THANK YOU SO MUCH, URUKA!
WE'RE GONNA CRUSH IT!
Hmph!
SNEAK
STARE
IF YOU'RE HERE TO SUPPORT THEM...
WHY NOT JUST GO OVER AND WISH THEM WELL, MAFUYU SENSEI?
EEK!
ZOOP
JOLT
KOMI-NAMI?!

NO, THANKS.
WHSH
THEY DON'T LIKE ME.
SO I'M SURE THEY WOULDN'T APPRECIATE THAT!
IF YOU SAY SO!
HUH?
NARIYUKI ISN'T HERE YET?
THAT'S UNUSUAL.
HE'S USUALLY THE FIRST ONE TO SHOW UP...
I'M SURE HE'LL BE HERE SOON.
THERE'S NO NEED TO PANIC YET.
ICHINOSE UNIVERSITY
...
YOU'RE OKAY, RIGHT...
... NARI-YUKI?
LICK LICK

EXAM GOOD
LUCK CHARM

Question 128:
More than Ever, What
Supports [X] Is...

[x] We + Never ÷ × Learn

THE NUMBER YOU ARE CALLING...
...IS NOT AVAILABLE OR IS CURRENTLY OUT OF RANGE...
ICHINOSE UNIVERSITY
NATIONAL EXAM
NATIONAL EXAM
YEP. I CAN'T GET THROUGH TO KOHAI EITHER...
YEAH. I'VE TRIED DOZENS OF TIMES NOW...
HIS FAMILY SAYS HE LEFT A WHILE AGO!
THIS ISN'T LIKE HIM. ON THE MORNING OF THE NATIONAL EXAM...
DO YOU THINK SOMETHING HAPPENED TO HIM?
LIKE WHAT ...?
SHIVER
WELL, ANY-WAY!

THERE'S NO USE IN STANDING HERE FRETTING ABOUT IT!

YOU THREE, GET IN THERE!

FOCUS ON YOUR TEST!

BUT... URUKA...

DON'T WORRY!

I'LL FIND A WAY...

...TO TRACK DOWN NARI-YUKI!

TMP
TMP TMP TMP
BUT ... HOW DO I DO THAT?
NO MATTER HOW MANY TIMES I CALL, I CAN'T GET THROUGH...

THE EXAM STARTS IN JUST 30 MINUTES...
...
8:58

SHOOOP
WAHH
THERE'S NO TIME TO LOSE!
I'VE GOT TO FIND NARIYUKI AS QUICKLY AS POSSIBLE!
SNIFF...
!

HUH?

WHFF WHFF

SNIFF... SNIFF...

OOOH!♡

WHAT AN ADORABLE DOGGY!!

WHERE DID YOU COME FROM?!

WAIT, WHAT AM I DOING?!

I'M IN A HURRY!

SORRY, GOTTA GO!

HUH?

WAIT A SEC...

TWITCH

WHA...
THE NA-
TIONAL
EXAM!
WHAT
TIME
IS IT?!

JOLT

ZONK...
KRAKLE
KRAKLE
DOOM...
NO!
THIS'S NO TIME TO BE SAD ABOUT MY PHONE!
I'VE GOTTA GET TO THE TEST SITE!

THROB

THROB
THROB
THROB
THROB
IT'S NOT ...
...BROKEN ...
DRIP
...I DON'T THINK ...
DRIP
GUH

SKF
SKF
SKF
SKF
SKF
SKF
SKF
SKF
SKF
I CAN'T JUST...
...GIVE UP ON MYSELF NOW.
WE'VE ALL WORKED SO HARD FOR THIS...
THROB
KOMINAMI SENPAI ...
OGATA ...
FURUHASHI ...
I HOPE YOU ALL MADE IT TO THE EXAM CENTER OKAY...
WHMF
!
SHOOSH

WOOF!

WOOF!
WOOF!
THANK YOU FOR BRINGING ME HERE, DOGGY!
IT'S ALL THANKS TO YOU...

AND TO THIS HANDKERCHIEF...
Big bro! You've got this! -Hazuki -Kazuki
You can do it, big brother! -Mizuki
Go for it! -Hanae
...YOU HAD IN YOUR MOUTH!

NARI-YUKI!
I FOUND YOU!!
You can do it, big brother! -Mizuki
Big bro!
ARE YOU OKAY? CAN YOU WALK?
I...
I'M SO SORRY, URUKA...
I HATE TO TROUBLE YOU...
DON'T BE SILLY, NARIYUKI!
IS YOUR FOOT REALLY OKAY?!
RRRING
!
FUMI-NOCCHI!
BZZZ
FUMINOCCHI
BIP

H-HOW'S IT GOING, URUKA?!
WE STILL HAVEN'T SEEN NARIYUKI AT THE EXAM CENTER!
FRET FRET
Women
PANIC PANIC
DID YOU FIND NARIYUKI, URUKA?!

OH! PERFECT TIMING, YOU TWO!
I FOUND NARIYUKI, AND WE'RE AT THE MIKAGE STREET INTER-SECTION RIGHT NOW!
ACTUALLY, NARIYUKI HAS A REALLY BAD INJURY AND...
KLIK
BEEP BEEP BEEP

WHAA-AAAT?! WHAT'S GOING ON?!
SOME-THING HAP-PENED TO NARI-YUKI?!
DA DA DA DUM

OH NO!
SHOOT! BAT-TERY'S DEAD...
Guess I drained it while I was search-ing...

THE TEST STARTS...
...IN 15 MINUTES...
WALKING AT A NORMAL PACE...
...IT WOULD TAKE 30 MINUTES FROM HERE.

THIS IS PATHETIC...
HOW DO I ALWAYS GET MYSELF INTO THESE PICKLES?
CAUSING EVERYONE STRESS AND WORRY AT A TIME LIKE THIS...
ALL OF OUR EFFORTS...
...GOING TO...
SKF SKF
...WASTE...

SKWEEZ
WE'RE GOING TO RUN, NARI-YUKI!

SEVEN MINUTES LEFT...
THERE'S NO WAY WE'RE GOING TO MAKE IT!

BUT EVEN SO...

IF SOMEONE IS THERE GIVING ME SUPPORT...
...THEN I'VE GOT TO GIVE IT MY BEST UNTIL THE VERY END.

EVEN IF I DON'T MAKE THE TEST...
...SOMEHOW, EVERY STEP WE TAKE RIGHT NOW HAS GOT TO MATTER!

12
3
6
TIK
URUKA ...
THANK YOU...
THANKS TO YOU, I...
BRRMMM

SKREE

WHAA-AT?!

PSHOOO

VREEE

WHAT THE—?!

QUICK!

GET INSIDE!

BAM

KI...
KIRISU SENSEI !?!

TEN MINUTES EARLIER ...

NATIONA EXAM

ICHINOSE UNIVERSITY

IT'S NO USE!

WE HAFTA FIND OUT WHAT URUKA WAS TALKING ABOUT!

Something happened to Nariyuki?!

LET'S GO SAVE HIM, FUMINO!!

DO YOU REALLY THINK NARIYUKI WILL BE HAPPY...
...IF YOU MISS THE EXAM BECAUSE OF HIM?!
OOG!
That's true...

WAIT, YOU GUYS! THE EXAM STARTS IN 15 MINUTES!

...

I MEAN, I KNOW ...

I FEEL IT TOO ...
FIDGET
FIDGET
FIDGET
GAH!
STUPID KOHAI! WHAT'RE YOU DOING?!
SEN-PAI...?
Hm?
NEVER MIND!
MORE IMPOR-TANTLY... YOU GUYS NEED TO...
WHAT A COM-MOTION!
WHAT'S GOING ON WITH YOU THREE?!
TMP
JOLT
!!
KIRIS SENS !!
...
...
YOU THREE NEED TO GET BACK TO YOUR SEATS.
FOCUS ON YOUR OWN WORK RIGHT NOW.
!
B-BUT... SENSEI ...!
I KNOW.

DON'T WORRY.

LEAVE THIS...

...TO ME.

BRRMM

I SEE.

SO THAT'S WHAT...

THANK YOU SO MUCH, SENSEI!!

...

YOU SAVED THE DAY, TAKE-MOTO!

HUH?

YOU TOLD FURUHASHI YOUR LOCATION.
ON THE PHONE.
AND ALSO ...
...YOU GOT YUIGA OUT ONTO A MAJOR STREET WHERE I COULD PICK HIM UP!
HON-ESTLY, WE WOULDN'T HAVE MADE IT OTHER-WISE!

Blush...
NOW, WE HAVE TO HURRY.
I'M GOING TO SPEED UP A BIT!
Hold on tight.
VROOOOM
AAAAAH! I KNEW IT!!
Y-Y-Y-YIKES!!

ICHINOSE UNIVERSITY

NATIONAL EXAM

TIK
TIK
TIK
TIK
TIK
TIK

BEGIN!

So, whose dog are you anyway?
Arf?
Pant! Pant!
Wanna come home with me for now?

Question 129: After Slushy Shenanigans, They Grow Closer to [X]

MY BROTHER'S OUT SEEING HIS DOCTOR ...
Heya, big sisters!
WHAT ?!
BRRMMM
I'M AFRAID I DON'T KNOW WHEN HE'LL BE BACK. YOU'LL HAVE TO STOP BY SOME OTHER TIME.
Except for Takemoto Senpai, of course! ♡
SKREEEE
EE-EEK! WHAT THE ?!
WAIT...
I'M GETTING DÉJÀ VU...
KCHAM
WHOA! WE'RE ALREADY HOME!
!

QUIVER
QUIVER
QUIVER
YOU REALLY TRANSFORM WHEN YOU GET BEHIND THE WHEEL, SENSEI!
I'm impressed!
WELL!
WHATEVER DO YOU MEAN?
ULP!
TH-THANKS, BOTH OF YOU, FOR YOUR HE—
BLRG!
OH DEAR!
I'M GLAD I DROVE YOU HOME IF YOU'RE FEELING SO QUEASY!
I THINK THAT'S ***WHY*** HE'S FEELING QUEASY!
KOMINAMI SENPAI!
AND KIRISU SENSEI!
HEY, LADIES!
I WAS JUST MAKING SURE KOHAI MADE IT HOME OKAY FROM THE CLINIC.
BAM
AND I JUST HAPPENED TO BE USING THE CAR FOR AN ERRAND ANYWAY...

ANY-WAY...
I KNOW I CAUSED EVERYONE A LOT OF WORRY AND STRESS ON THE DAY OF THE EXAM.
I'M SORRY.
THANK YOU ALL SO MUCH FOR YOUR SUPPORT.
SHEESH, KOHAI! YOU HAD US ALL WORKED UP OVER A SPRAINED ANKLE!
IF OUR SELF-ASSESSED TEST SCORES SUFFERED, WE'D HAVE TO PUNISH YOU FOR MAKING A MOUNTAIN OUT OF A MOLEHILL!
Gah!
Ha ha ha!
YEAH! BUT WHAT A RELIEF...
SEN-PAI...
RIZU AND FUMINO...
ALL OF YOU SEEMED TO HAVE DONE WELL, RIGHT?

!
REALLY?!
U-URUKA, SHUSH!
YOU BLEW OUR BIG NEWS!
Oops!
SO... HOW...
...
...WAS YOUR TEST, NARI-YUKI?
HUSH...
BAM

YAAA-AAY!!
WAY TO GO, NARI-YUKIIIII!
AUGH!
AAA-AAH! NARI-YUKIIIIII!
HEY, HE'S INJURED! DON'T TACKLE HIM, YOU TWO!
WAIT FOR ME!
Phew...
KIRISU SENSEI!

COULD I RIDE IN YOUR CAR...
...AGAIN SOME-TIME?!

RIZU-RIN AND FUMINOCCHI, YOU SHOULD REALLY EXPERIENCE THIS TOO!
SHE'S ALL, VRROOOM, SKREEE, BRRRRRMMM! IT'S WILD!
SHP
WHOA!
URUKA?!
FIDGET
FIDGET
...
...
I'M IN A HURRY.
I'D BETTER BE GOING NOW.

SPLAT
AUGH!
TEE HEE HEE! ♪
WHY NOT BE A BIT MORE HONEST, SENSEI? ♡
CACKLE
CACKLE
FWIP
KOMI-NAMI ...
GROW UP, WILL YOU?
SHOOP
OH!
PAFF
WHSH
MISSED ME! ♪
DRP

THIS MEANS WAR!
GRRR
OH YEAH?! BRING IT ON, RIZU-RIN!
HEY, EVERY-ONE, CALM DOWN...
HLRFF?!
I SAID, CALM DOWN!!
NGHA!
HEY...
HEY NOW!
PAFF
CUT THAT OUT! THIS IS OUR GARDEN!
WHO THREW THAT?!
GRR
WHOA! ARE YOU IN TOO, MIZU-KIN?!

PSST
WHAT ARE YOU STARING AT, KOHAI?! ♡
YOU PERV! ♡
Heh...
HUH?!
I-I-I WASN'T!!

I WAS JUST GETTING A LITTLE EMOTIONAL...
IT'S JUST SUCH A BEAUTIFUL MOMENT...
EEK!

COLD!
I'M GETTING SNOW INSIDE MY CLOTHES!
OOF!
OOF!
NO FAIR! I WAS ALL OUT OF BALLS!
OH, NO!
MY BOT-TOM'S ALL WET!

OH, YEAH?
EMO-TIONAL, HUH?
A BEAUTIFUL MOMENT?
YOU SLEAZY PERVDOG!
PSHHH

I TOLD YOU, THAT'S NOT IT!
AWW, JUST OWN IT! ♪
YOU MIGHT BE KINDA PERVY, BUT I ACCEPT YOU, KOHAI!
STILL, I HAVE TO TEASE YOU ABOUT IT! ♡
STOP!

...

What are you all doing?!
And you too, Mafuyu?!
DRIP DRIP
WE'RE SORRY...
...FOR-
FOR CRYING OUT LOUD!
ALL RIGHT, ALL OF YOU! INSIDE, NOW!

SHAH

WELL, THIS IS INFINITELY AWKWARD!

HOW DID WE END UP LIKE THIS?!

INTO THE BATH WITH YOU! NOW!
IN THAT CASE...
WE'RE NOT VERY WET, SO...
THE THREE OF YOU SHOULD GO FIRST! ♪
Heh heh
URUKA AND SENPAI...
...ALWAYS SCHEMING!
Guh...
!
POKE
...
FIDGET
...
UM...
KIRISU SENSEI...

SPLASH

THANK YOU SO MUCH!

!

WHA...

WHAT'S COME OVER YOU TWO?!

? ?

THE OTHER MORNING, SENSEI...

THANK YOU SO MUCH FOR RESCUING YUIGA!

LEAVE THIS TO ME!

I DON'T KNOW WHAT WE WOULD HAVE DONE WITHOUT YOU!

I SEE NOW...

...THAT I MISJUDGED YOU.

I ALWAYS THOUGHT YOU WERE COLD-HEARTED.

I'M REALLY SORRY...

...I'VE BEEN SO RUDE TO YOU.

WE'RE ...
...REALLY SORRY.

I ALWAYS THOUGHT...
...THAT PEOPLE ...
...HAVE TO PURSUE THEIR TAL- ENTS TO ACHIEVE HAPPINESS.

I THOUGHT IT WAS MY JOB AS A TEACHER TO STEER STUDENTS IN THAT DIRECTION.
AND THAT IF I LET THEM GET OFF COURSE, THEY WOULD WIND UP UNHAPPY, LIKE ME.
EVEN IF THEY RESENTED ME FOR IT...
...I FELT THAT IT WAS...
...MY DUTY.

AND I PUSHED MY SELFISH BELIEFS ...
...ON YOU TWO.

BUT OTHERS HAVE HELPED ME TO UNDER-STAND...
...THAT MY BELIEFS WERE WRONG.

AND YOU TWO...
...ARE LIVING PROOF.

I'M THE ONE...

...WHO OWES YOU BOTH AN APOLOGY.

I'M SO SORRY!

SZZ
SZZ
SZZ
HERE, SENSEI! HAVE SOME KIN-CHA-KU!
ISN'T MIZUKI A FANTASTIC COOK?!
FAWN
FAWN
HERE, SENSEI!
HAVE SOME DAIKON RADISH!
E-ENOUGH!
I'VE HAD PLENTY! YOU TWO, EAT UP!
SHEESH... THAT WORKED BETTER THAN EXPECTED.
AND SO FAST.
HM...
YOU'RE AWFULLY QUIET, KOHAI. WHAT'S UP?
PERVING OUT AGAIN?!

STARE
BLOOSH
?!

DADADUM
COME ON, SENSEI! HAVE SOME PIPING HOT CHIKUWA !!
WHAT ARE YOU DOING, RICCHAN ?!
I WAS GOING TO OFFER THAT TO SENSEI!
OOPS!
SWIP
SHLOOP♥
#@$*@#!!
Yikes! That's gotta burn...
FUMINO AND URUKA GOT A PRETTY STERN SCOLDING AFTER THAT...
...BUT AT LEAST RECONCILIATION WAS ACHIEVED!

I hope...
...that didn't leave a mark.

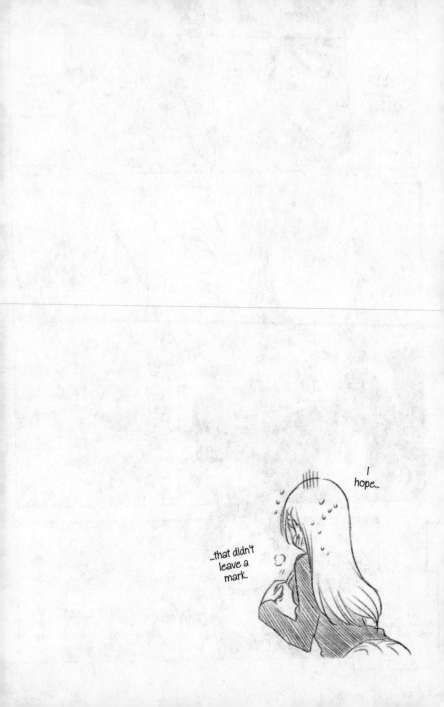

Question 130: Sometimes a Genius Still Struggles with [X]
LOVE
LOVE

[x] We + Never ÷ × Learn

一ノ瀬郵便局
ICHINOSE POST OFFICE
POST OFFICE
AWWWWW YEAH!
APPLI-CATION SUBMIT-TED!
ALL DONE!
NOW WE JUST HAVE THE SECONDARY TESTS AT THE END OF FEBRUARY.
ALL WE CAN DO IS STUDY WITH EVERYTHING WE GOT!
WELL, IF THAT'S WHAT'S HAPPENING, FIRST OF ALL...
GRRRWLL
SUPER KAWAI
LET'S GET SOME LATE-NIGHT MUNCHIES...
I MEAN, SHALL WE STOP FOR GROCERIES?
I HEARD YOU SAY LATE-NIGHT MUNCHIES, FURU-HASHI!

SUPER KAWAI

ARMACY

PHARMACY

大根
58円

FRESH VEGETABL

OH...

TREMBL
TREMBL

GUH
GUH

白菜
598円

WAIT... I'M GETTING A SENSE OF DÉJÀ VU HERE...
WOW, KIRISU SENSEI! YOU'VE GOT A LOT OF BAGS!
IT'S MORE EFFI-CIENT THIS WAY.
I TRY TO BUY MY GROCERIES IN BULK...
RRRRRIP
OH NO! YOUR BAGS!!
PLOPPH PLOPPH
I KNEW IT!

THANK ...
THANK YOU BOTH FOR HELPING ME...
DO YOU HAVE TIME FOR A CUP OF TEA BEFORE YOU GO?

OHHH! ARE YOU SURE?
OOOH?! ARE YOU SURE?!
HMPH!
WHY THE INCRED-ULOUS TONE, YUIGA?

BUT HER APART-MENT'S ALWAYS IN A STATE OF DIS-ARRAY!!
KCHAK

SPARKLE
SPARKLE
SPARKLE

WOW! IT'S LOVELY!
WHAT A BEAUTIFUL SPACE, KIRISU SENSEI!
?!

WOW, SENSEI! I'M IM-PRESSED!
BETWEEN THE NATIONAL EXAM AND MY INJURY, I HAVEN'T BEEN BY IN A WHILE...
WELL, OF COURSE!
Such a grown-up apartment!
YOU HAVE A LOT ON YOUR PLATE.
I CAN'T KEEP LEANING ON YOU FOR SUP-PORT...

FWAAAAM
FWUD
FWUD
FWUD

HUH?!
WHAT WAS—
?!
SHP
WHAAAAA?!
WHAT ARE YOU DOING, NARIYUKI!?
This is hardly the place...
S-SORRY, FURUHASHI! IT'S AN OUT-OF-SEASON MOSQUITO...
THIS IS KIND OF A WEIRD WAY TO REACT TO A MOSQUITO!!
SHUV
S-safe!

SKRIT
SKRIT
SKRIT
SKRIT

CLEAR THE MIND.
FORGET ABOUT YOUR RESULTS ON THE NATIONAL TEST.
THE TASK AT HAND IS TO MAXIMIZE YOUR SCORES ON THE SECONDARY TEST.
SKRIT
SKRIT
SKRIT
SKRIT
OUR FOCUS IS ON PRACTICE TESTS FOR YOUR TARGET SCHOOLS...
...AND ELIMINATING ANY CARELESS OVERSIGHTS IN YOUR WORK.

FURUHASHI, FOR THE MATH EXAM FOR THE S.T.E.M. DEPARTMENT AT TENGE UNIVERSITY, YOUR TARGET SCHOOL...
...YOU CAN GET PARTIAL CREDIT ON QUESTIONS IF YOUR REASONING IS CORRECT.
SO DON'T GIVE UP ON PROBLEMS THAT YOU CAN'T COMPLETELY SOLVE.
R-RIGHT, SENSEI!

TEE-HEE...
GETTING SUPPORT FROM SENSEI IN MY CHOSEN FIELD OF STUDY...
...FEELS REALLY GOOD!

AND IT'S ALL THANKS TO NARIYUKI...
NOW, WHERE WERE THOSE TEATIME SWEETS I HAD?
THEY'RE IN THE TOP CUPBOARD ON THE RIGHT!

There they are!
MATCHING MUGS
GUEST CUP?
LOVE
LOVE
LUNCH-TIME...
HUH...?
I JUST HAPPEN TO HAVE STOCKED UP ON GROCERIES ...
?!
OH!
YOU'RE USING THAT APRON, SENSEI!
KTUNK
BAM
...SO I'LL MAKE CURRY!
You can study while you're waiting!
YES, I FEEL A BIT STRANGE ...
...BUT SINCE YOU GAVE IT TO ME...
UM ...
SEN-SEI...

WHAT'S BEEN GOING ON BE-TWEEN THESE TWO?
I'M GET-TING A WEIRD FEEL-ING.
DA DA DA DA DUM
I'LL MAKE IT!
W-WHAT'S THIS?
GUESS THEY'RE BOTH BEING EXTRA NICE BECAUSE OF THEIR RECENT RECONCIL-IATION!
NO, LET ME!
DUM DA DA DA DA
Heh heh... WELL. THAT'S SWEET!
SOME-HOW I FEEL A STRANGE URGE TO COMPETE...
ALL RIGHT!
IN THAT CASE...

SHOOP
SHOOP

WE'RE ABOUT TO FIND OUT...
...WHO MAKES A TASTIER CURRY!

LEAVE THE CURRY TO ME! ♪

FURU-HASHI, YOU CUT YOUR FINGERS!

SPURT SPURT

THEY'RE SPURTING BLOOD!

AUGH!!

?!

THE BEST THING IS TO WASH THE CUTS IN COLD WATER!

PSHAAA

BADMP
BADMP
DISIN-FECTANT KILLS THE GOOD BACTERIA ON OUR HANDS TOO!
IF YOU CAN KEEP THE WOUNDS FROM DRYING OUT, THEY'LL HEAL FASTER...
BADMP
BADMP BADMP

OH!
BADMP
BADMP
BADMP
BADMP
I-I'M SO SORRY! I DIDN'T REALIZE I WAS LEANING UP ON YOU!
I was just trying to balance...
R-RIGHT... YOU HAVE THAT INJURED ANKLE ...
I-IT'S REALLY OKAY...
STARE

OH!
WHAT AM I DOING?
I LOST MY FOCUS THERE ...

LET'S SEE... THE NEXT STEP...
DO I TURN OFF THE BURNER? OR TURN IT UP?!
OH DEAR... I CAN'T REMEM-BER...

RUMMAGE
RUMMAGE

WIGGLE
WIGGLE

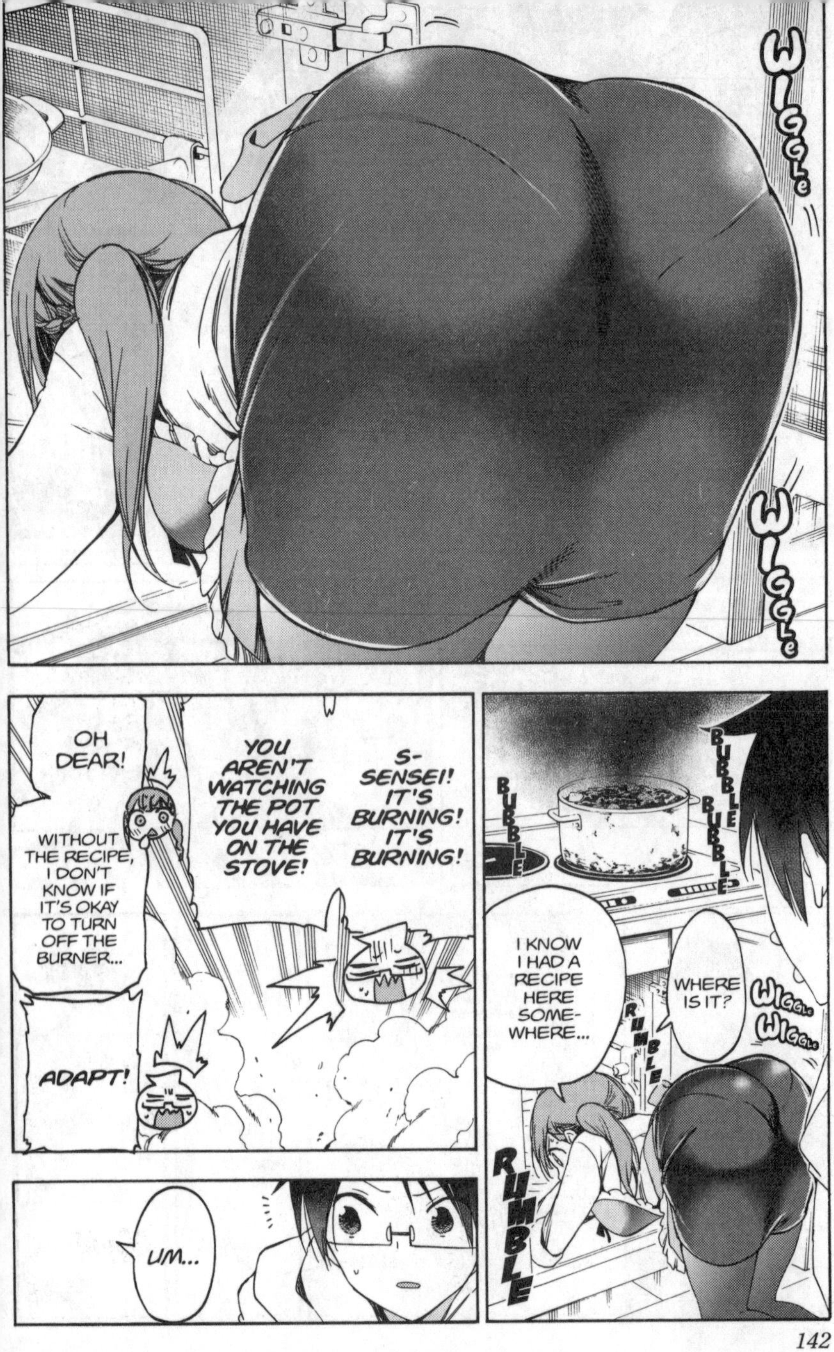

BUBBLE BUBBLE
BUBBLE
BUBBLE
WHERE IS IT?
I KNOW I HAD A RECIPE HERE SOME-WHERE...
WIGGLE
WIGGLE
RUMBLE
RUMBLE

S-SENSEI! IT'S BURNING! IT'S BURNING!
YOU AREN'T WATCHING THE POT YOU HAVE ON THE STOVE!
OH DEAR!
WITHOUT THE RECIPE, I DON'T KNOW IF IT'S OKAY TO TURN OFF THE BURNER...
ADAPT!

UM...

FIRST I SAUTÉ THE MEAT AND VEGETABLES IN OIL...
BLUB
BLUB
BLUB
I WONDER...
...HOW MUCH OIL?

DOOM...
UM...
ARE YOU TWO...
Okay?

DIS...

DA DA DA
DIS-GUST-ING!
YOURS TOO, SENSEI!
THIS IS DISGUST-ING!!
FOR A MOMENT, I SAW LIGHT AT THE END OF THE TUNNEL!
DUM

HOW ODD!
DA DA DA DA
I MIGHT SAY THE SAME OF YOU!!
YOU SEEMED SO CONFIDENT!
...
DUMMM
NOM NOM
MIHARU

THANK YOU BOTH FOR PUTTING SO MUCH TIME AND EFFORT INTO THIS FOOD.

NEXT TIME...

...IF YOU CAN MANAGE TO BE FRIENDLY AND WORK TOGETHER, THAT WOULD BE GREAT!

AGREED.
BUT, FURUHASHI...

SOME-HOW...
MURMUR
YOU ALWAYS MANAGE...
...TO SAY JUST THE RIGHT THING.

I THINK THE FACT THAT YOU ARE SO ALIVE AND ENGAGED...
...IN MY PRESENCE...
...IS ALSO THANKS TO YUIGA.

LET'S TRY AGAIN!
AND THIS TIME, LET'S WORK TO-GETHER!
I'LL LOOK UP A RECIPE!
WHAA-AT?!
Again?!

MIMARU

MM!!

DADADA DA DUM

DELI-
CIOUS
!!

I CAN'T BELIEVE HOW BIG A DIFFERENCE IT MAKES TO BE CALM AND CENTERED!
MAKING CURRY IS A LOT LIKE STUDYING FOR A TEST!
WHOAAAAA!
OH, FOR PETE'S SAKE!
HA HA HA!

FURUHASHI HAS A SUPERHUMAN TOLERANCE FOR SPICINESS!

Wel-
come
home,
big
brother!
We're
having
curry
tonight!
An extra
big serving
for you!
ROUND THREE!
KLANG

Question 131:
Sometimes Their [X] Is Flexible

...
WHAT'S GOING ON?

A LITTLE WHILE EAR-LIER..
SKRIT
SKRIT
SKRIT
SKRIT

OUCH ...
OW... MY SHOULDERS ARE ALL STIFF!
WIGGLE
KRAK KRAK
WELL, YOU'VE BEEN WORKING NONSTOP SINCE THIS MORNING!
KOMINAMI SENPAI WILL BE HERE SOON. SHALL WE TAKE A LITTLE BREAK?
GASP
WAIT! RIZU OGATA!
PER-HAPS YOUR SHOUL-DERS ARE STIFF...
...BECAUSE OF YOUR BREASTS!
WHAT ?!
SEKI-JO!
WOULD YOU MIND NOT SHOUT-ING BR... SHOUTING THAT IN MY HOUSE?!
I'm glad my family's not home!
YOU DON'T GET IT, NARIYUKI YUIGA!
BREASTS CAN BE A HEAVY BURDEN!
STOP SAYING BREASTS!

WELL, I HAVE TO AD-MIT...
WE'VE BEEN STUDYING A LOT AND NOT MOVING OUR BODIES ENOUGH!
PLUS, MY FOOT IS INJURED...
HEH HEH!
I KNOW JUST THE THING, NARI-YUKI!
SHOOOP

STRETCH-ING, HUH?
URUKA RECOM-MENDS IT!
I'M TRYING TO MAKE A HABIT OF STRETCHING DURING MY STUDY BREAKS!
Gah...
O-O-OW...
GUH GUH
YES, YOU'VE GOT A WAYS TO GO, NARI-YUKI!
SHEESH! I'M SO STIFF!
THAT RE-MINDS ME...
I WAS REALLY STIFF IN THE BE-GINNING TOO.
BUT IF YOU STICK WITH IT, IT PAYS OFF!
I REALLY RECOMMEND DOING A LITTLE BIT EVERY DAY!
See? Like me!
UM, YOU HAVEN'T MOVED A MIL-LIMETER!
I'M PRETTY SURE YOU AND I ARE IN THE SAME BOAT!
TRMBL TRMBL TRMBL

HUH?
WHAT?
SHOOP
DUMMM
WHAT ARE YOU TWO LOOKING AT?

SEKIJO, YOU'RE AMAZING!
COACH SEKI-JO!
PLEASE INSTRUCT US!
HUH? COACH?!
I LIKE THE SOUND OF THAT!
BLUSH

BUT IF YOU TWO ARE THAT STIFF...
YOU MIGHT FIND IT MORE EFFECTIVE TO DO PARTNER STRETCHES.
BUT I DON'T REALLY KNOW A LOT ABOUT PARTNER STRETCHES ...
HOW COME ?
SWIP SWIP
I GUESS BECAUSE I'VE NEVER HAD...
...A FRIEND TO STRETCH WITH...
DON'T WORRY! I'LL STRETCH WITH YOU, SEKIJO!
ME FIRST, NARI-YUKI!
NO...
YOU TWO HAVE TO STRETCH TOGETHER! THAT'S THE WHOLE POINT!
NOW... PRESS DOWN FIRMLY ON HIS BACK!
Thanks anyway!
O-OKAY...
PRESS PRESS
NGHH!
NOW, SIT BACK-TO-BACK AND TAKE TURNS BENDING FORWARD!
SLOWLY OPENING UP THE SHOULDERS AND LOWER BACK...
MM...
AH...
TUGGA
GEE... THIS IS KIND OF STIMULAT-ING!
BADMP BADMP BADMP
OKAY... NEXT... ARMS ...
LEGS ...

YEOOWWW!
TUGGA
KREAK
LIKE ...
LIKE THIS ...
POP
POP
SEKI-JO?!
THWAK
THWAK
HFF
AAAGH
Is this a real stretch?!

SHF
HEY!
SORRY I'M LATE, KOHAI ...
HAD TO STOP BY CRAM SCHOOL AND...
BLOOOOSH
... LEADING US TO THE PRESENT MOMENT!
WHAT'S GOING ON?

SKRIT
SKRIT
SKRIT
SKRIT
SKRIT
TIK
TIK

MY NOSE WON'T STOP BLEEDING, SO I'D BETTER HEAD HOME!
GOOD BREASTS! I MEAN, GOODBYE!
BLOOSH
I HOPE SEKIJO'S OKAY!
Why's her nose bleeding?
WELL, AT LEAST OUR BODIES GOT WARMED UP!
I FEEL A LOT BETTER!

...
SLIGHTLY FLUSHED AND SWEATY
BREATHING HEAVILY
NARI-YUKI...

SHP
I'M NOT SURE WHAT RIKIYA IS FEELING IN THIS PASSAGE...
SLIGHTLY PLUNGING NECKLINE...
YUZURIHA UNIVERSITY PAST EXAM QUESTIONS

YOU TWO SEEM TO BE GETTING REALLY FRIENDLY!
HUH ?!

SEEMS LIKE YOU WERE HAVING A PRETTY GOOD TIME TOGETHER JUST NOW...
AM I WRONG?
WINK♥
OH, WE WERE JUST PARTNER STRE...
YES!

IT WAS GREAT.
IT REALLY TOOK MY MIND OFF STUDYING.
WE HAVE DIFFERENT EXPERIENCE LEVELS...
AND AT FIRST IT WAS KIND OF AWK-WARD...
HEH
...BUT THEN IT FELT SO GOOD!
STARE
...
WOW!
?
UM...
ARE YOU... ANGRY ABOUT SOME-THING?
OF COURSE NOT!

JUST...
KICK
I'M IMPRESSED YOU MANAGED ALL THAT WITH YOUR INJURY!
YEOOOWCH!
OOPS! SORRY!

ARE YOU OKAY, NARI-YUKI?
PAT PAT
HERE, LET ME PAT YOUR HEAD AND MAKE YOU FEEL BETTER!
Krik!
HUH?!
I'M OKAY, REALLY!
WEIRD...
DADADADUM
IT REALLY DOES SEEM LIKE SHE'S ANGRY ABOUT SOMETHING...

MASTER FURU-HASHI!
WHAT ON EARTH SHOULD I DO NOW?
Tee hee!
Figure it out...
...yourself!
Gasp
UM...
SEN-PAI...

COULD IT BE...
...THAT YOU'RE JEALOUS?
WHAT ?!
WHAT DID YOU JUST SAY, KO-HAI?!
KOMI-NAMI SEN-PAI...
IF THAT'S WHAT'S GOING ON, YOU COULD HAVE JUST TOLD US!
NOT YOU TOO, OGATA!
I DON'T BELIEVE THIS!
OH, NOW YOU'RE PAYING ME BACK FOR TEASING YOU, HUH?
NICE TRY!
BUT YOU'RE NO MATCH FOR ME, KIDS!

I WOULDN'T TEASE YOU ABOUT SOMETHING LIKE THIS!
BAM
EEK!

I...
...CARE ABOUT HOW YOU FEEL, SENPAI!
WILL YOU...
...LET ME...
...DO IT WITH YOU TOO?

I DIDN'T ...!
I MEAN, I WASN'T TRYING TO...!
I'M NOT READY...!
SEN-PAI...
LISTEN!
NO!
BLUSH
YOU'RE YOUNGER THAN ME!
I CAN'T—

I'M NOT—

TUG

HERE!

HM ...?
HM?
HM?
TUGGA
TUGGA
TUGGA
Me next!
HOW'S THAT, SENPAI?!
FROM NOW ON, ONE OF US WILL ALWAYS STRETCH WITH YOU!

Ngh!

OH.
I'M REALLY SORRY.
BUT... WHAT'S GOING ON?
WELL...

I FIGURED YOU WERE JEALOUS BECAUSE WHEN YOU WERE IN SCHOOL...
...YOU DIDN'T HAVE ANYONE TO STRETCH WITH EITHER.
YOU'RE REALLY ASKING FOR IT NOW!
HUH?!
What did I do now?

THAT DUMMY!

INTERRUPTING OUR STUDY TIME WITH THAT NONSENSE!

WELL, SURE, BUT...

At least we managed to focus and get some work done after that!

IN THE END, WERE WE WRONG...

...ABOUT YOU BEING JEALOUS?

YOU WERE WRONG!!

BLUSH

Tee hee!

...

YOU'VE CHANGED ...
...YOU KNOW THAT?
I THINK YOU'VE CHANGED TOO, SENPAI!
Hmf!
YOU'VE BECOME MORE APPROACH-ABLE.
YOU'RE ONE TO TALK!
BUT ...
...IF THAT'S REALLY TRUE...

IT'S SOME MORON'S FAULT.

YES.

IT MUST BE SOME MORON'S...

... FAULT.

BY THE WAY, SENPAI ...
WHEN YOU SAID, "I'M NOT READY..."
WHAT DID YOU MEAN?
BLUSH
FOR-GET IT!

Eek!
Bloodstains
What happened while we were out?!

Question 132: On the Dusky Riverbank, She Finally Rows to the [X]

WOOF!
WOOF!
WOOF!

EASY!
YOU'LL WEAR YOURSELF OUT!
WOOF!
YOU SURE HAVE LOTS OF EN-ERGY!

HALT
SNIFF SNIFF SNIFF SNIFF

SHOOSH
WHOA!
WHERE ARE YOU GOING?!

YIP!
YIP!
!
OH! NARI-YUKI?!
URUKA?!
YIP!
YIP! YIP!
PANT
PANT
LICK
LICK
LICK
YOU'RE OUT AND ABOUT EARLY TODAY!
HOW'S YOUR LEG?
MUCH BETTER!
I'VE BEEN SITTING AROUND SO MUCH LATELY. I NEEDED TO MOVE A BIT!
It was really hurting last chapter!
HEY, YOU!
WHERE'S YOUR FAMILY?
YOU REALLY HELPED US OUT ON EXAM DAY!
SNIFF

THANKS FOR LOOKING AFTER HIM, URUKA.

NO PROBLEM. I LOVE DOGS!

BUT...

I HOPE WE FIND HIS FAMILY...

...SINCE I'LL BE GOING OVERSEAS SOON!

...

MEI-KAKU-NA!

NOT BAD, HUH, NARIYUKI?

BAM

WOW!

YOU'VE REALLY LEARNED THOSE!

IF YOU KEEP THIS UP...

IF YOU KEEP THIS UP...
I'LL BE GOING OVER-SEAS!

What's the next word?
SPAC-ING OUT, NARIYUKI?
WAVE WAVE
OH!

?
OH!
UM... WELL...
KOFF!
C-
GOOD! WE JUST HAVE TO MAKE SURE...
...YOUR SPEAKING IS SOLID...
THERE'S AN ENGLISH INTER-VIEW, RIGHT?
YOU'VE GOT TO STAY SHARP!

WHH
STROKE!
STROKE!
STROKE!
SHHHH

SHP
BOAT RENTALS
WHSH
WHSH
WHSH
WHSH
WAIT UP!!
STROKE!
STROKE!
STROKE!
SHOOSH!
HERE, NARI-YUKI! LET ME ROW TOO!
STROKE!
STROKE!
WHOA! THEY'RE FAST!
Are these guys pro rowers ?!
WE'RE LOSING THEM!!

BOOF

YEEK!
SORRY, NARI-YUKI!!
MFF?!
GMFFL MFFL MFF!
EEE! ♥
TWITCH
D-DON'T TALK NOW!

H-HERE!
LET'S WORK TOGETH-ER AND ROW!
OKAY, HERE GOES!!
Sorry...

OH... UH...
IS THIS OKAY?!

NOOOOO!
WE'RE NOT CUD-DLING!
I DON'T SMELL ANY-THING!
SHOOP SHOOP SHOOP
WHAT?!

UM...
<Let's see...>
<Excuse me. We want to...>
YAP
<Look, Rick! It's that cute couple again!>
YAP
HA HA HA
<Let's leave them alone, Damian! We're interrupting their date!> ♡
YAP
YAP
<Good point!>
YAP
<We don't want to interfere! Let's go!>
YAP
TWITCH
<Oh, um...>

W-WAIT!!
SHOOOSH
<So long! Have fun!> ♡
<Aww!> ♪
SHOOSH
SHOOSH

?!
SHA SHA SHOOSH

F-FANTASTIC!
OH MY GOD!!
HUHHHH?!
WHERE'D THE TURBO SPEED COME FROM?!
UH... WE'VE PASSED THEM NOW!!

HUH?!
SAY WHAT?!
WHSH
PSHOOO
NOW YOU'RE OVER-HEATING!
WHAT'S COME OVER YOU, URUKA?!
Stop!

<Dog?>
<Y-Yes!>
<Please give us back our dog!>
<Did you see a dog?>
<No...>
<I didn’t see any dog when we got off the boat...>
GASP
DON’T TELL ME... IN THE CONFUSION...
IT FELL?!
<Please!>

<He's about this big!>
<He has shaggy eyebrows and brown and white fur!>
<Please tell me anything you know!>
<And he has a funny face!>
<And his breath smells kinda bad...>
OH~...
HUH ?!
<Your English is very good!>
OH! UM... THANK YOU...
UH... THAT'S NOT THE ISSUE NOW!
<So, you mean...>
<...that handsome guy over there is your friend?>

OHHH!
OHHH!
LOST DOG
Name: Kotaro
Description: Good-looking Distinctive Eyebrows
LOST DOG
Name: Kotaro
KO-TARO!
I'M SO GLAD TO SEE YOU!

I'M SO SORRY I DIDN'T WATCH YOU BET-TER!

DON'T EVER RUN OFF AGAIN, KOTARO!

YIP!

YIP!

YIP!

WAGGA WAGGA

DID THAT DOG JUST LEAP ASHORE FROM A MOVING BOAT?

THAT WAS AMAZ-ING...

Psst

Psst

BAM

I SEE ...

HE JUMPED IN THE BOAT TO GET BACK TO HIS OWNER!

Boing

Boing

WHAT A DRAMATIC PER-FORMER!

For some reason, that kid looked familiar...

WELL, ANY-WAY!

SHE WAS SO HAPPY!

Thank you, big brother! Big sister!

WE FOUND HIS OWNER!

YEAH ...

TRUE.

SHALL WE HEAD HOME?

TAK

THAT WAS MORE RIGOROUS EXERCISE THAN I INTENDED!

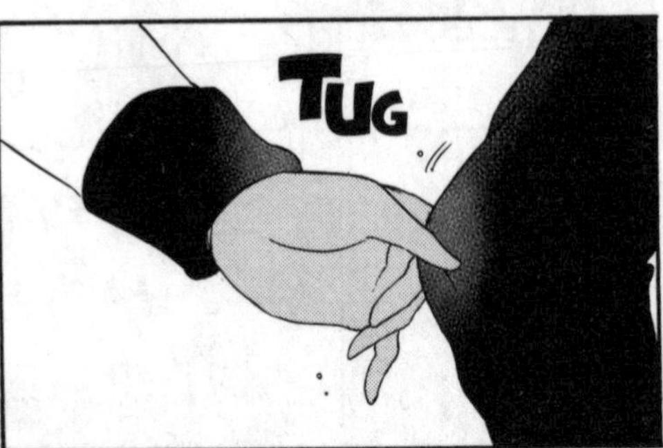
TUG

IT GOT ...
... PRETTY CRAZY.

WANT TO ROW SOME MORE?

...I CAN ACTUALLY SPEAK...

...SOME ENGLISH NOW!

YEAH!

THAT'S TRUE!

HONESTLY, I WAS IMPRESSED!

YOUR PRONUNCIATION WAS GOOD TOO!

YOU'VE REALLY WORKED HARD!

HEH HEH!

ALL RIGHT!

IT'S SOMETHING TO CELEBRATE.

SHE'S PROGRESSED A LOT TOWARD HER DREAMS...

MORE THAN I EVER EXPECTED.

WELL, I GUESS THAT WRAPS THAT UP.

BUT...

IT IS A LITTLE SAD.

FOR SOME REA-SON...

...I SAID THAT...

... WITH TWO MEANINGS IN MY HEART.

THE NEXT DAY...
Yip!
Yip!
What?! Again?!
Go on home, Kotaro!
You'll make your owners cry!

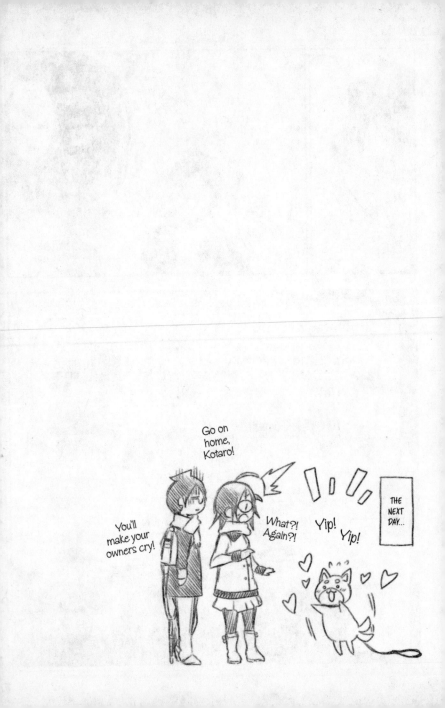

We Never Learn 15

STAFF LIST

Taishi Tsutsui

Yu Kato

Naoki Ochiai

Sachiko

Yukki

Satoshi Okazaki

Paripoi

Chikomichi

[x]
We Never Learn reads from right to left, starting in the upper-right corner. Japanese is read from right to left, meaning that action, sound effects and word-balloon order are completely reversed from English order.
1
2
3
4
5
6
7
8
9
142
Teacher?
NONO
tempow